The Mystery of the Hidden Driveway

Jennifer L. Knox

The Mystery of the Hidden Driveway

BLOOF BOOKS

"Let's go out and shoot some ducks."

—The dying words of John James Audubon

For Dad, Marilyn, Gobi & Loop

I.

Gene Kelly Sings to the Cow

and anything else he can get his mouth up to—
the heather, the glen, the toe shoe, the camera
lens he opens wide to swallow whole. "Listen
to me sing everything," he tells it in his stomach
but it's a camera, not a microphone—an eye
not an ear—and all it sees in there is red, red
like rage, like the blood filling Debbie Reynolds'
tap shoes, always having to be right, even the left
tap shoe, tantrums on the tennis court.... The "Bully
bully bully for yoooou" whooed through thin lips
to the munching bovine just before he shoves it over
only *sounds* like love, unlike the thud of the beast
who knew in the pit of all four stomachs that
the crooning loon was lying through his loafers.

MARRIAGE

All year, crawling home from bars—through snow, rain and sweat-stinging summer nights. But in August peonies began to beckon me from the kept yards of houses we'd never own because we couldn't keep money in our pockets, because we were always going to bars, because we never cared for the quiet work of caring. We stuffed ourselves fat on clutter and glitter—on meat and beer and Mardi Gras beads—taking in and in but never taking care. How did such blowzy flowers manage to come back after nine months of bitter winter? Tough blood. I'd steal them whether in full fluffy bloom, or still in budlike fists. The bright fibrous stems were a bitch to sever, even with my teeth. Many times trying to boost a bouquet, I yanked a whole bush out by the roots. He'd stand on the sidewalk with a dark smudge for a face and say, "You know what's gonna happen." And I did. I'd carry home the flowers I'd risked getting busted for, not trim the stems at an angle, fill a vase with water and a pinch of sugar to keep them fresh, and arrange them high to low like children in a class photograph. Instead I'd dump the lot in a heap on the kitchen table, pass out in my clothes, and snore all night like a pig. The next morning, we would wake to a million ants pouring from the flowers, down the rusty table legs, and onto the wine-spotted rug. Ants are the fingers combing the Filofax pages that are the petals of the peony. I could've left them to live, to thrive beside a house—maybe with a little girl inside who made up stories for the flowers about princesses in feathery skirts, but I didn't. I killed them, then stuffed the seething, gorgeous things into the trash. I could've planted my own outside our rented house, heavy with dead Christmas lights, but I didn't know how to grow things then. I still don't really, but it's rare I get drunk enough to tear up someone else's garden.

THE FATTEST WOMAN I EVER LOVED

was a contralto who drove birds to suicide. Frantic to plunge themselves down the source of her sound, they'd hurl themselves at her lips which were pitted with scars, and her spherical shadow was peppered with bits of broken beak. I wanted to see Voice, but I only saw Fat. She'd wear a black tent with a neck hole cut in it and stand far behind other people in photographs, which made her look like a ventriloquist dummy. She spent the night once: Her footsteps on the stairs made the whole house wheeze like a Borscht Belt comic's accordion. From her nest of blankets on the sagging couch she kept waking me up to do impressions of animals where she came from. Sandusky—did I mention that? Her donkey made me laugh 'til tears poured down my furry face. I hadn't laughed like that sober in a dog's age. She would've reminded me of my mother, if I'd have let her.

BELLE WITH A SHOWY, RED LEAK

It was tough to poke the thick embroidery needle through
her lower lip and twist the stud in before the hole closed.
Lips don't want holes in them. Same with tongues.
She'd have to be more gentle in the shower
than she'd ever been with anything—brush the blood
softly away as if with someone else's sleepy hand.
Whitney was coming over to do her hair, with wine coolers
and straws. She'd cut all her nails so she wouldn't snag
her new black tights when she pulled them on drunk.
Nothing covers bruises like black tights. But all that would
come later: the bruises, the buzz, the busted nuts, her
getting shoved listlessly from one set of hands to the next
like a beach ball the whole crowd's tired of hitting.

"COFFEE ICE CREAM AND FRUITY PEBBLES,"

Big Don at the downstairs desk says to me
as I pass with a handful of cookies—a suggestion,
I think—what to eat next if I find myself
hungry for more crap. "You're Fruity Pebbles,"
I say over my shoulder and pause, suddenly
unsure how all six feet seven inches of him
will react. "I love them things," his bass voice
booms. Big Don's always been real nice to me,
but Sam told me one night Don cornered him
and said, "I love kissin' on fat little white boys
just like you," which scared the shit out of Sam.
When I told Cammie about the anger
management class, she was shocked. "Why
did you have to take that?" I told her exactly
why, and she said, "Whoa! I had no idea!"
and I was so proud of myself that I'd kept my own
secret safe all these years from someone
who didn't need to know it—not until all
the damage I'd needed done was done.

The Clean Underwear/Ambulance Thing

When I was 12, I had sex with my
stepmother. It was fantastic,
and not a bit weird. I mean it.
You think maybe I wouldn't know
as I was just a boy, but I was a boy
who would've known, and it wasn't.
It was fantastic.

Any man in town would've given his hand
up to the thresher for a crack Marianne,
despite her withered leg: The purple swirling
stripes and throbbing varicose veins rivaled
my own pulsing boyhood boner.

I've spent the rest of my life searching
for a like leg. I've painted its portrait over
other legs, babies, jobs...all for naught.
Finally I took up tanning, which is

fantastic too. I'm so good at it,
people can't believe it when I tell them
I'm 10,000 years old.

"M" Is for the Tears of Meat She Shed Me

Yes, we raised a crocodile as one of our own. The herpetologist from the community college said it would never survive, but it thrived!

Kevin, as we called him, slept at first amongst the kittens, then we moved him to a makeshift bed amidst balls of soft angora yarn in Grandmother's sewing basket. How heavenly to watch his luminescent scales rise and fall as he dreamed away—his sour breath whistling through his snout as through a piccolo. He always joined us at the table, and shared our simple Quaker diet, eating and drinking from a child's pink plastic plate and cup set.

Then mating season came, and we were sleepless with worry that Kevin would leave us to follow his nether urges. But nothing could have been further from the truth: Kevin laid a single speckled egg about the size of a fist and that was the end of that. This story ran in newspapers around the world.

At Christmas, he crawled in the crèche and worshiped at the feet of the wooden infant alongside wise men and sheep. We have no photographs of any of this—just crayon drawings the children made.

I remember well the wintry night Kevin's mother knocked on our door. She claimed she had accidentally left one egg behind that fateful day she moved her clutch in fear of wolves. Father asked, "What is your name, Madame?" "Uh, Alice?" she said but we could tell she was lying. "Alice, your behavior is unnatural," he said and closed the door. We watched her out in the yard a long time through binoculars as snow fell around her, a bit of something else's skin clinging to her chin.

DARTING UNDER THE WALL OF WATER

a wave made of water
a wave made of salt water
a wave made of salt
of salt that once was sugar
of sugar our President silver-spooned into his tea
of sugar that lined our President's pockets
of sugar cubes that once made up our President
sugar cubes made our President up
sugar once upon a time then candy for kids
kids laid in the grass eating candy
glowing yo-yos and hula-hoops dozing nearby
poison clearly marked on the bottle with skull and crossed bones
one house per family
one family per house
houses made of cut trees and fired bricks
houses made of poisonous meat and poisonous soap
vegetables made of poisonous sugar
families made of people growing sicker
people growing sicker in different directions such as
alone with a plastic bottle of antibacterial soap
when the going gets tough: antibacterial soap
the going's got a whole lot of plastic going on
plastic instead of candy (the candy'd always been plastic)
before plastic all candy was a coconut
we opened the coconuts with swords
many someones died to test the swords
a three-torso sword, a four-President sword
we smuggled out a recipe for the metals in our blood
a wave in the blade where the metals won't mix

SEABIRDS

Sundown: I was pantsless, stranded with gimpy Ma and gaunt Granny in a bombed-out station, waiting on a train that wasn't ever coming, but I needed to protect them from that bare, hissing wire of information. Sure, we were going to die, but would we lap at the blood pumping from the throats of our own like hogs? Bikers with tattoos hidden between their fingers grabbed their nuts and barked. Faded families huddled around trashcan fires. Then I was topless, clutching closed an unraveling towel. A biker *whoop!* went up. *What lovely seabirds!* Mother said of the sick things suddenly all around us in the air—eelesque, hissing through teensy fangs, wingy fins rolling like the hem of a flamenco skirt, skirting too close, sizing us up. *Don't touch those!*—I called to my women—*They aren't seabirds!* One brushed my arm, but I dared not flinch. Instead I chanted *I hate seabirds* in my head and held my breath, which I was so good at, my held breath held the cracked concrete together all the way down the empty platform, 'round the bend, down the dead line far as I could see, 'til I could see no more but seabirds.

Red/Green Color Blind Madness

Whoa there, Stretch. Hands
off—the madness stays right
where I left it, Pokey warned,
holding a purple gun on me.
See it's a philosophy, really—
a conscious choice to be this way—
though it's costed me dearly...

It's rabies, you dolt—you're
drooling all over the place,
I said, feeling the spider's egg
buried in the hump on my head
jump. Soon it would hatch
and its scorching righteousness
would pour forth like lava.

BATTLE OF THE NETWORK STARS: "DREAM TEAM"

She asked if she could
sing a song for us
in the bathroom.

It was about love,
a lover,
life,
and being Irish.

The sound in the stall:
like she'd opened
a box of wasps
onto our faces.

Later we laughed about her song
as we were charging the fattest
hooker in the stable
on a credit card we stole
from my mom's purse.

OLD FRIENDS

I'm in a coffee shop, remembering a woman I knew
years ago who had drowned eight kittens in a sack.
I listened to her tell the whole story many times, even
begged her to repeat it when we were wasted, and laughed
at the part where the flung sack hit the concrete instead
of the water. I'm thinking how different things are now,
especially me, how my heart can barely stomach the story,
which means I've become a better person, certainly better
than the woman I knew, who I would never be friends with
again—she probably hadn't changed at all. Now that I'm
a better person, I probably shouldn't forgive her, or
should I? I wonder, and as I'm wondering this, the bodies
of all the people I'd drowned in sacks years ago begin
falling from the sky, heavy like wet sandbags from a crane.
I go out to watch them. God, lots of them. To each, I
wave as it flies past, mouth "I miss you," wait for "Me
too!" from the back of its smooshed, hairless head.

Saving Her Wasted Breath

It was a surprisingly easy find at 5 AM in Anaheim,
but I'd be less a sore thumb in clown drag: a bruised boob
with a broken nose in a new white suit (pulled the tags
off with my teeth). Goofy. If those Canadian pigs get ahold
of me, they'll beat me 'til their knuckles bleed for kicks.
Mongoloid Todd's a tougher fit—the gate was locked
at Len's Big and Tall, so I threw his blood-soaked duds off
the pier and he climbed in the trunk bare-ass—been there
two hours. When I gas up, I'll cop us both T-shirts and shorts.
Even back there, his psycho talk's louder than the radio. God
only knows what he's got in the golf bag. Better burn it.
Marina warned me how the border guard's rotts troll
from car to car like sharks, smelling through their mouths,
so keep the windows open all the way to Surrey. And that
was it. No shit she never sapped out and said *Stay,* but
the *Go to hell*s and *You stupid fuck*s and all the rest I never
earned but deserved—nix on those sweet nothings too.

ANOMALIES OF THE FEMALE REPRODUCTIVE SYSTEM

"It's time for you to get a mammogram."
"Yeah, I know, but I don't have insurance."
She laughs once, hard, like a punch. "Let's try that
again. It's time for you to get a mammogram."
Pause. "Uh, I don't have the money." She *pffts.*
"Yes, you do—you're not on welfare. Ask your
parents. And why haven't you had a Pap smear
since 2007?" "Because I don't have any insurance.
The lab bills cost $200. If I get a Pap, I can't pay
my rent...my parents are...I'm 41 years old...it's
on my chart..." Huge *hunf.* The sharp edges of her
rings under the gloves twist and tug the latex like teeth
biting through. "Does that hurt? It shouldn't!" "Uh
yeah—it does, actually. Not bad, but it's uncomfortable...
it's creepy." "What's so creepy?"   You're so creepy.
"A plastic brush scraping back and forth across your cervix
is creepy, and I'm sure I'm not the only one who thinks that!"
"Well, you're certainly the only one who's ever voiced it!"
Right then in walks Mary McDonnell—the actress who played
the mom in *Donnie Darko* and Kevin Costner's girlfriend
in *Dances with Wolves.* She's wearing an organic cotton
lab coat and cushy Wallabees. "Hi, Jennifer. I'll be your
new gynecologist, and I agree with you one hundred percent:
A plastic brush scraping across your cervix is creepy, indeed."
Mary and I use lasers from the *Battlestar Galactica* series
in which she played the President to slay the old doctor
and cut up her body. Then we feed the pieces to the hawks
in Central Park. It's a gorgeous day for turning that
cuntless cunt into birdshit. After that, Mary buys me
ice cream. I eat it while she smokes. Then we float
over to the lagoon and race those little toy sailboats.
She wins, but insists it's a tie.

of what an intervention was—of how one might proceed—of the wailing throngs gathered to beg at her fixed, filthy feet—but especially of what she'd be wearing (a flak jacket over a taut black tank—or a frayed denim miniskirt, laceless hightops and an XXL Thrasher hoodie—or the coup de grace: rearing at the end of their lassos like a wild mustang in just her little tits, no panties, and chaps (though she'd have pawned anything leather long ago—but that's why they're called dreams)) were but dreams.

Grandma, Grandpa, Uncle Ed (drunk as fuck—ain't that some shit) and Junie, her best friend from fourth grade who was now a big fat loser, nabbed her scabby ass at a fake birthday dinner at TGIFriday's wearing old lady stretch pants she'd found at Marco's mom's condo and a stained polo shirt straight out of the dumpster. Didn't even get a bite of her birthday sundae which she actually might've finished. She hopes they got sweats or flip-flops out in the desert—Chapstick at least, for which she throws in a quick prayer, ending it, "in Jesus' name, Amen."

II.

CARS

The house was far enough away, as big as another big bush across the desert, when Dad announced it was my turn to drive the old truck. I said I didn't want to. I cried. But he wouldn't hear no. He scooted the seat all the way up and we switched places. I stretched my tiptoes down to the pedals and took off way too fast while he shouted things: *Shift! Turn! Slow down! Look out for the hole, God damn it! Look out for the God damn hole!* I hit the hole hard enough to blow a tire, knock the battery off its cage and all the radiator hoses loose. Walking home together, through my cried-out puffy eyes, I could still see the unending wave of the crimped, gray steering wheel, could still feel the torn, plaid upholstery itchy beneath my bare legs, can still feel it.

Dad bought a '66 Corvair, parked it in the driveway, and left the keys on top of the refrigerator. My girlfriends and I cut school, went to my house, got stoned, then suddenly it hit me. Duh. "Let's go for a ride," I said, jingling the keys. We bought wine coolers at the liquor store that would sell to us when we pretended to be foreign exchange students, and drank them at the aqueduct. On the way home, about a mile from the house, the car died going up a hill, so we got out, pushed it the top, jumped in and coasted down into the driveway, right into the same spot my Dad had parked it. The mechanic told him the transmission had been blown—no fluid. I denied knowing anything about it, just bald-faced lied. Twenty-five years later, that car is parked in my brother's garage. Weekends, he works on it with his 16-year old son. Sometimes the kid comes home after school and shammies the whole shebang without being asked, even all the greasy little bolts, until every bit shines.

Starting at the top of Godde Pass after dark, not one streetlight along the hairpin mountain road, he'd cut the motor and steer with his knees, gaining speed for miles downhill, all the way home. Everything was silent. Reflecting light on their white wings, moths whipped in and out of the headlights like paper snowflakes. Only the whirling, open *ah* of the wheels. The occasional crunchy *thunk* of a pothole hit. "Don't tell your mother," he'd say. "Why?" "Because this is fairly dangerous." "Why?" A long pause. "If a deer jumped out in front of us, we couldn't stop." I loved deer, and he knew it. We were closer to the cold still stars above us than the glowing houses whipping by in the canyon below. He'd turn the motor back on as we pulled into the driveway, then turn it off again.

Coming around the bottom of Quartz Hill Mountain Road drunk on Halloween night, I took a sharp turn way too fast, skidded on the sand, jerked the wheel too hard and hit a telephone pole.

Coming home stoned, way past curfew, the garage door slowly lifted and there he was—standing in the door in his blue bathrobe. A surprise! Not altogether bad. I knew he would try to make my life hell, but it was nice to see him out of his room for a change, as if he cared, as if he could still make something happen, or stop something from happening. Maybe he really could. Maybe this was the beginning of a whole new deal. But I pulled in too close to the fat metal coil holding the garage door up. The sound of a shrieking pterodactyl as the spring sunk its teeth into the front fender. But I didn't stop, for some stupid reason. I kept crawling in slowly, our eyes locked, my brow crunched in concentration, his jaw slack as the coil gouged deep into the car all the way to the bumper. I couldn't imagine what he was going to do to me when I turned the engine off and got out. But he only asked, "What the hell's the matter with you?" and shut the door behind him.

He drove home twice with broken noses, 85 miles, from his hockey games in L.A. He didn't even ask the medic to tape them, just drove home with blood all down the front of his jersey. He never stayed home sick from work a single day that I can remember. On Sundays, the only day off work he gave himself, he, a hypoglycemic, would fast.

Traci and I racing home from the prom over Godde Pass: her in front in the Chevette, me in the BMW doing 70, taking the hairpins at 40. We knew every turn (there was one you didn't dare try over 20), the sun coming up across the green valley far below, some cows. I thought, "Fuck boys," and, "Hey, we could really die." For an A-student, Traci was a batshit driver—flipping me off, mouthing in her rearview mirror, "…you…pussy…you…"

Returning from a Sunday morning beer run, still drunk, a mere two blocks from the apartment, going 60 in a residential housing tract, I tried to pass a van full of Girl Scouts on the left and rammed into their passenger door as if hurled by giant slingshot. Monty, my copilot, took off running back to the 7-11, yelling, "We're gonna need gum!" The mom driving the van sat with hands gripping the wheel—gulping, hyperventilating, hysterical—until the dad ran out and herded the little girls into the house like a SWAT team hostage evacuation, "Get in the house! Go! Go! Go!" Then he turned and pointed right at me, "You're a fucking idiot!" I couldn't have agreed more. "I'm calling the cops!" They took an hour to show up. By that time, between the adrenaline and swallowing two packs of Tropical Punch Bubble Yum, I must've seemed sober. I told no one about the accident. My dad got a letter from his insurance company weeks later, but I'd already gone back to college. Later that year, I flunked out.

The month I was born, he was driving back from work very late. He could fall asleep anywhere, even when he was driving—his head lolling around on his long thin neck (we found out years later that his sinuses were so packed with polyps from his allergies, it was amazing he could get out of bed—he must've been exhausted and in terrible pain for years, the doctor said). We lived up the road from an old folks' home. The night nurse said she never saw the man walk out the front doors and into the road. Everyone was supposed to be asleep. The doors were supposed to be locked. Dad drove over a blind hill, hit and killed him. Mom made Dad write an apology to the old man's daughter who lived in another state.

I blew a tire coming home from a Dead show in L.A., but because I was tripping I kept on driving—60 miles on the tiny inflatable spare. A car pulled alongside me flashing its lights, rolled down the window and yelled, "You got a shower of sparks coming off your wheel! That spare's gonna blow!" "It's cool but hey thank you man!" I made it home, woke up the next day, still wasted, late for class at community college where I was taking a full load of courses to get my GPA up from a .08. I'd forgotten all about the tire until it blew, rounding the first curve of Quartz Hill Mountain Road as The Fall song "Bremen Nacht" was playing. The car swerved like a cat on ice skates. And it's true: Your whole life does flash in front your eyes. It happens really fast but every detail's in there, even the stuff you've forgotten. The car drove off the cliff, turned in the air, and landed 30 feet below upside down on top of a Joshua tree, its sharp green spines like saw blades thrust through the shattered windows. I ended up in a ball behind the passenger seat with nothing but a tiny scratch on my hip. Oh, how I mourned those shoplifted pants the EMTs cut off me.

Smoking crack for the first time on top of Quartz Hill Mountain road, I managed to hand the pipe over my shoulder to David before turning back to face the wheel and hitting a different telephone pole.

I could never predict when he would get angry. But since his happiness was rarer, maybe I should say I could never predict when he would be happy. On Sunday, we'd go for long rides all day. One time coming home from church, he was angry at me about something. The car was hot. I wanted to fall asleep but I knew if I did he'd cuff me for sure. He hadn't spoken a single word for hours, then he pulled over and asked, "Do you know why you do the things you do?" He left the motor running. I knew that meant he didn't think it would take long. I also suspected that there was no right answer. And I was right.

He said, "I want to sign you up for driving class out at Willow Springs—it's a stunt driving class. They teach you how to take jumps, and do 360-degree turns with one pull on the wheel...and some other things." Long pause. "I don't think that's such a good idea, Dad." Every car he gave me to drive—right up until the last one, an International Scout—"malfunctioned" in a major way. Breaks went out, axles broke, tires blew. So how stupid would I be now not to think, "Maybe he was trying to kill me"?

Father-Daughter Day. He pulls over on the side of the Hollywood Freeway and sobs. "I'm sorry. I've worried about you so much. So much more than your brother...." I have never seen him cry, but he really does. He bawls. I say, "It's OK," and I mean it, because suddenly I know, he's just scared. That's why he did all the things that he did.

Going to back to college in the fall, but until then, off to work. My head's clear. The back axle breaks when I'm doing 75 on a straightaway. The car flips three times, ending up in the ditch facing the opposite direction with the roof flattened to the seats. Once the EMTs cut me out of the car, nothing's wrong, but they take me to the hospital to be safe on a stretcher in a neck brace—my first neck brace and stretcher. When he arrives at the hospital, Dad asks, "Is someone paying you to do this?" and we all laugh, even the nurses. Mom keeps repeating the phrase "jaws of life." They're divorced by this point, and there's something nice about seeing them there together, for me. This accident feels different from the others. It's sunnier in my mind. It made me understand that it wasn't just me being a fuckup—it was the car—it's all the cars.

III.

YELLOW TRACES

Red for cars, yellow for a lady's dress, said Dad
on one of our long drives when I asked his favorite color.
I didn't know you could have more than one.

A good story: Once stopped for gas on Laurel Canyon,
Steve McQueen pulled up on the other side of the pump
in the same Porsche. Dad's was red, Steve's was yellow.

Mom never wore yellow, nor would the new wife
who writes: Yesterday he saw three kids in yellow
swimsuits playing in the backyard who weren't there.

Beloved Canadian Sandwiches

Candied ginger, walnuts, and cream cheese on white with the crusts cut off's what they served after church in the facility. I drove an hour there and back for a crack at just half.

Cherries (but should be berries—wild ones—everywhere—spilling out in bushels from bushes growing in ditches) and margarine or somesuch.

Leave it to the left-behind to linger on things they believe the leavers left for (bananas, avocados).

Congested Donald in Meat Cove writes: Dijon mustard and horseradish in a #10 envelope.

Canada's #1 export is envelopes.

Most passed on the smoked salmon and salted sour cream on black bread and went straight for the lunchmeat. It was once we had so much of things from the sea they was steeped in tea 'til no one could stand the sight of them. Imagine. Now that even Canso's clean fished out and dead. Nothing's along that long drive out to the point but crows.

The Prime Minister's a Mary: fat-free potato chips atop date squares.

Anything with dates on account of how they travel: years alone at sea.

Anything with Mary on account of how she you-know-whats.

So many places, fished out and dead. Even the fish. Even the dead.

With Dad, it was molasses. Steak burnt black. A grapefruit half, crunchy across its surface with sparkly sugar—like the ice rink at night.

Tea-poached chicken and dressed watercress on wheat so burly it slices the roof of your mouth up like too much dry Cap'n Crunch (which is cheaper by the box than a pint of wild berries, picked from a ditch bush).

Baking bread took all day—it used to be a wonderful thing not to have to bake your own. But then, the bread...

Ruth poured cream on everything but margarine (which now grows on trees).

Anything that traveled well from Canada (not Ruth).

Salami, mustard and pickles. Cucumbers'll grow anywhere (but that's what they said about salmon).

Leave it to the leavers to linger on the things they left behind (which, from there on out, stand still: no such salmon since, etc.).

So many they's fished out.

BEVERLY HILLS COP III

This again, but way lamer. We started out
outlaws, now we're law (in chichi suits, yet).
Why does every bright, rare thing we are boil
out like wine's kick in a simmered port glaze,
leaving only virgin vapors, Ghost of Badass?
Like this: The synthesizer—formerly a wink, sweet
mystique—thunders now, boops and stomps around
as hammy as a Scottish soccer anthem. The walk-on
waiter and his foppish lisp have sailed from sidelines
to sidekick—shares every scene, gets his own
badge, his own girl, his own fight and fall.

HOUSTON

Stickier than Saigon itself, Mom said on a visit she cut short. One hundred and one by 8 AM when a man wandered up to our yard sale and asked if we had any guns, knives, bows and arrows, Chinese throwing stars, nunchucks, etc. My apartment was a converted garage with two skinny windows that let hardly any light in. Under the sink was a big hole you could see outside through, and AstroTurf on the bathroom floor that never dried. I sat in the top turret at the Orange Show late one night tripping with Winnie who got the key from his girlfriend who worked there and hated my guts. House of Pies, House of Lies. The old shrew who owned the Aquarium Lounge made her sad boyfriend sleep on a sheet of plywood laid across the pool table. Stanley asked if I wanted to see a body after school and warned me never to drive through the neighborhood after dark. I was cruel to Oscar and I still regret it. I also hurt Bruce with the lisp: The last thing he said to me was, "OK, OK, I get it." The neighbor was an older Allman Brothers-looking dude who gave me a ride to the airport once after my car had broken down again. I said something about Mississippi John Hurt and he said, "Now you're talking, baby." I think I wanted to have sex with him. Am I invoking catastrophe when I say that, twenty years later, having been a vegetarian in that smoldering kingdom of broken glass and charcoal pits is one of the greatest regrets of my life?

One Man's Trash

Right after Nothing but Gunpowder died
at the ripe age of rage, and piece by piece
of him had all shut down like bagpipes,
his wife, Forget It's Forgotten, forgot how
he'd hollered on and on about the crops:
scrub plants, but their sap contained aspirin—
just pluck one and suck the stuff out.
Forget It's Forgotten swore chewing on
the leaves put her to sleep better than beers.

Then the rain stopped. So she forgot the rain.

Lifetimes ago, Nothing had kissed her over
and over in the long house—she felt love
in his lips and hands and he kept on. Charcoal
on Snow, a lovely dancer, was watching them
from behind a curtain. She would always remember
how seamless they seemed, one thing wound
of two like rope—up in each other's pockets.

Forget It's Forgotten had long forgotten all of this.

THE MULES OF DEATH VALLEY

Hauling bone-white borax up from the hellish Harmony
Mine Works in July. Each on the train, the end

of its line. The end, mule. *Ya.*
How sad. Soft ears and whip-

cracking clever, drivers said.
Patient. Affectionate. Loyal. Beloved.

Ho, best of donkey. *Ha,* best of horse.

They can kick in all directions but won't
willy-nilly. Ideal companions for lone

prospectors plodding past Badwater's tease,
past the thin, unhinged shacks of Rhyolite.

There [he spots two specks—another
man and mule—maybe a half day's off].

Why would God give such gifts to an end-
of-the-line animal that loves only this world now—

loves only those of this now—the ones mad
enough to leave green homes and farms for Furnace Creek?

There're no others to love.
Both are the ends of their lines.

For years Scotty blabbed about a mine so deep
it went clean through the earth.

The only other set of eyes to ever fall upon it were
a mule's.

Why give soft ears where God's grace
melts fast as ice?

A Coyote Walks into a Quizno's

How gameless must've been the plains
to drive it through the traffic of Chicago.
How flat-out busted to muster nonchalance
and sidle by a winding lunch crowd line seeking
handouts from predators and curl up by a cooler
in the dead-end back. Too bushed to shrink
from our hunger's sour scent. Giving up,
closing in, or had it snapped—seen itself
a son, prodigally lying down among its like?
'Til Animal Control arrived, serene—green
eyes low, but not deferred—primed to parley:
"From one hunter to another, brother,
spare a scrap? I'll get you back."

LOST FEET SWIM IN BACKTRACKS RETRACED
After Kubrick's The Shining

In the book, there were bees. Here, no need
when catacomb patterns in vines vein-blue
and withered-red slither up the walls instead.
Labyrinths run the long hall rugs' weaves.
While color schemes morph from sealed wing
to wing, the season doesn't budge. Just like
you, Coyote: mazes within, mazes without. You:
born for grander stuff—radiant roughneck—stud.
Hansel and Gretel got you down? Sticking out?
Stinking? No sweat. You see through mountains'
lidless eyes: dancing under the snow, a rich girl
dressed in a rabbit mask and furs. You alone know,
though the light's icy, her warm guts are green
(and the mask's a game, but its teeth are real).

FAT CATS, SKINNY RATS

The Japanese feed peas to goldfish swimming upside down
which takes hours, but the green balls get gas out which is why
they swim wonky, or so says my employer. That, and
the love rat he gave Frau Kunstkrank's the toast of Stuttgart.
That, and he'd pay handsomely for a rare albino love rat—
a renowned French geneticist offered him one, then reneged
as my boss isn't a certified testing lab. "Such credentials
are easily forged," I mutter, slink home, unchain
the basement door and listen to the common ones—
soon to die unnamed, unsung—flee the reaping light.

Babies in Silent Movies

How'd they make it cry so loud?
You know under the ragtime roll's
a wail that'd peel paint, can see
the blond brows crimped like claws
beneath the gingham bonnet, cheeks
red hot despite spectrumlessness.
Maybe a lackey's pinching its thigh
under the table. A good mother'd
shrug off the short pricks of pain one
outgrows to keep a kid back then that fat.

VILLAINS IN SILENT MOVIES

A poor farmer could be turned into one
by the brunette slinking past his falling
fence each night on her way to the wicked
city around the corner. The lake you rowed
your chittering wife out on's at the end of your arm.
Just reach out and tap it, or her temple, once
with the oar. Brunettes were eviler than blonds.
All brunette was all black. All farmers were poor.
Farmers who turned into villains were killed
like the loving wives they'd murdered.
Villains who started out the movie villains
were also rich, stayed rich, and faded away
once the better-lit victim was healing in bed,
flanked by family and a blurry gray daisy.

MODERN POETRY

Mostly grey clouds, same color
as battleships, suburban Seattle.

In the bottom left corner: a clown—
his red nose, a sudden start, or

stoplight. Only his comic prosthesis
is clear—the rest's a blur (everyone

gave up on faces in the 80s—too hard).
The clown ends at neck—his body

fades to clouds. Then, like a ghost,
in the center: white outline

of a bitchin' 70s muscle car,
hood popped. Its centrality

and size suggest deep feeling.

Questions for Discussion
1. Look at the clown under a magnifying glass. What is the word that best describes his expression? Type the word in your blog. Does that word change when you smoke pot?

2. If you were standing in the poem, would you be wearing a T-shirt or a parka?

3. The airplane on which you are flying home to visit a dying loved one (but can you really love at all? what good is your love?) suddenly loses a wing and begins plummeting towards earth. What do you grab on the way down: the cloud, the clown, or the muscle car?

4. When was your last good kiss, and why?

Burt Reynolds FAQ

Burt Reynolds is the son of six grizzly bear brothers and the Holy Goddess of Cherry Trees. He was born from his mother's nose, which ensures lifelong charisma. Before he could walk, alligators would gather to watch him wrestle other babies. He excelled at all sport, especially football, baseball, gymnastics, rugby, tennis, archery, swimming, sailing, and horseback riding. At school, he was not the brightest student in the class, but he was the luckiest; whenever the teacher called upon him, he would guess the answer correctly. When he was seven, he grew his first mustache. Wealthy older women fought for the privilege of combing it through with gold paint. He was made a general in the President's army, but on the eve he was to leave for battle, robbers clobbered his knees with a tar-covered club. Burt was crushed because his knees were crushed, but he never cried. The President's queen said, "Stay here and read me stories," because he was also the most talented storyteller in the land. So he rose to great power, which made the priests and princes jealous. After the night a murderer poured mercury into his ear as he lay sleeping, he became The Lion Who Did Not Want to Be Loved. But the people would not let him not be loved. Neither would Burt be pinned. The match is still going—no one knows who will win. At night, Burt returns to his home on the edge of a fire pit with a lush green yard full of tigers waiting for him to read them a story, like the old days. Burt does not believe he'll have no need for toupees in heaven. In summer, his mustache still grows unruly with lily of the valley.

DEAD ITALIANS

In the back of my mind—in the back of my freezer—
two different freezers in two different apartments
for nine months—the time it takes to have a baby—I've carried
three pounds of sausage—spicy Italian sausage—homemade
in Milwaukee—sausage capitol of Planet Earth—carried
them home on the plane last July—stowed them still fresh
in the overhead bin two hours and have carried ever since—
from apartment to apartment—from summer to winter and
nigh onto July again—and sometimes I'd say to no one—to everyone—
Hey! I got spicy Italians from Milwaukee in my freezer—
but today I thawed them out and they'd gone bad—I could tell
by the smell, so the song says—probably'd been bad all this time.
So the allegory comes of itself: Frozen food is imagined
food and therefore lives only in the mind. To treasure—even
love—that which lives only in the mind is to love nothing
'til the beloved of the mind becomes flesh—steps from the mist
and suddenly you're dancing with your love—arms wrapped—
torsos grooved together like tongue tip to envelope flap—you think
at last but then you smell death—your lips never touched but
already long dead. Now imagine a violin braying as the lover
dips you dangerously low—then lower—wouldn't that make
a great opera?

IV.

Don Ho's Funeral

Between sighing deep, nostalgic *wahs* of aftersex, the steel guitars *oingy-woing*ed and lolled around the altar torches. Seventy-six round-armed, caramel-colored beauties stood beside seventy-six lifesized photographs—one for every year of his lei-draped life. At 2: riding a wild boar coaxed from its cave by his golden coos and babble. At 17: flashing his hominy-white teeth that lit a secret path for mainland girls sneaking to his bungalow at night. In every decade: smiling with his arm around a tourist's stooped, white shoulder, for Don Ho would take a picture with anyone—no matter how fat or awkward—free of charge. Great shaman Mickey read the eulogy. Mickey'd only come down from his hut on the volcano's slope one other time: the 1969 moon landing. Mickey told us many things we'd never known about the man Don Ho, the husband Don Ho, the father Don Ho—and one thing we did: Don Ho was a really good guy and everybody liked him. Now Don was nestled in the always-86 degrees, breezy bosom of the Lord where everybody's gonna get paid, everybody's gonna get champagne—the good stuff—with tiny bubbles zipping off like pricked balloons, like cells unwinding in the blood.

The Earth Is Flat and So's My Ass

These days, not so much regret. Brute will's broke
as a petting zoo pony. Funny how it kept us entranced
by difficult piffle that passed as the whole enchilada.
Bruises always fresh as hothouse violets—they dared
not darken to the ochre that signaled surrender and
whatever came next. We called it not "Delusion"—more
like "Man Gnaws Off Limb in Tractor Accident."
[Gavel pounds] But gentlemen, we believe something
has [big time] shifted, that you won't catch us again
marching stiff and shatterable as stale candy canes
into a taco stand to demand our just potato kugel.
We accept all [llllll] the limitations. We understand
the work will be [deep sigh] arduous—the toads to be
swallowed [burp], numerous, and [hoo!] it's gonna get
ugly [er].

DIRTY HARRY'S CHRYSALIS

It's cool. Your sand-colored hair suffers
the punk's gritty spit but just a sec [simmer].
Such affronts throb like bamboo under the nails.
The kid and two other toughs unsheath their knives,
bring bony knees to your corduroyed groin [simmer
what seems eons in the scalding insult soup
that sits like a pig made of pepper on your chest].
No greaseball like that lives to walk away [so...?].

In the future David Lee Roth will become fluent
in Portuguese, pass the NYC EMT exam, chatter
hours on satellite radio about how much he loves
people, and finally—despite speculations as to his
sexual orientation—become the President
of the United States of America.

CRAWLING OUT OF THE MOUTH OF MORE

If we start tying each other up,
fucking with buttplugs in, fisting,
having three-ways, three-ways with fisting
and buttplugs, four-ways, pussy vacuums,
penis pumps, nipple clamps, assless chaps,
drinking each other's piss and all that shit,
will we fuck more or less? Will we be capable
of fucking without all that—you know, just a
nice fuck? Just a quickie? I know real people
don't fuck like people in movies—we're shier
and fatter—but if we started fucking all nuts like that,
I bet we'd have to leave regular fucking behind,
leave it waving bye-bye at us from the shore
like a mute, shoeless waif. But that might be OK.
Maybe we wouldn't have to leave it—maybe we'd
get to, and never look back—except in the mirror
at our own lube-soaked, flog-streaked asses.
Have you ever seen that website with ER X-rays
of weird stuff people have unfortunately tried to
insert in their butts? Lightbulbs, pepper grinders,
Mrs. Butterworth's bottles, hammers, high-heeled shoes,
Ken dolls, umbrellas, unexploded WWII artillery shells....
My favorite: the man who'd poured wet concrete
in his anus and waited for it harden before his lover
drove him to the hospital. I took a sculpture class
in college: Concrete grows startlingly hot just before
it hardens, like a bad idea before your own strange
hand shoves you in its whirling blades.

THE ATOMIC WEIGHT OF GRUDGES

Some bad patches break down
slower than quartz—dumb-
ass Marge who said one thing
one time—you remember.
No? Hmm. 'Kay—guess it's all
on me to keep the rage torch
flaming hot enough for two
to roast s'mores on—for us,
darling, which I deeply resent.
But notice how that resentment's clog
drains slower than the pain of the 3-way
Jägermeister enema—which was all
my "brilliant"* idear.

*New York Post, page 69, Thursday, October 14, 1994.

YOU ARE A STRATEGY

You are a strategy
for to get what I need.

You are a little left-
over cheese in a baggie.

You are a bad strategy.
Are you a purple skirt?

Then thanks for the child-
hood (flowers) I never had.

Actually I got flowers every
Valentine's Day (violets).

You are a strategy to get
what I never got as a

childish purple skirt.
I was spoiled rotten.

That was their strategy.
It was a bad strategy.

You're actually pretty
cool—the unbending way

you claim your baggie.
I don't know how to

balance my checkbook.
Never learning how

is a strategy that takes
lifetimes to pull off.

I am a baggie of bloat. Ironically
that's one empty baggie.

I fear the end of many
bad strategies: Those

who spoiled me are dead:
Who will tell me stories

of the flowers I actually got?

You're F*cking Crazy

I found him in the backyard at midnight
wearing a foam rubber sun costume—no tights
or underwear on—one ball hanging out the leghole
like a jawbreaker in a baby sock. He'd dug all the
bulbs we'd planted back up and was scrubbing them
skinless with an SOS pad. Music blaring on the stereo:
Christmas bells over TV snow.

"Hey. You're crazy," I called from the window.
"Nah, I had free air from the hose at lunch," he told the tree.
"No—over here—you're crazy." At last he saw me.
Nostrils flared, "No! You're crazy!" "Nope—you're crazy,"
I volleyed, knowing he'd go for broke. "You're F*CKING crazy!"
he blasted, which woke up Mike, the white poodle in the shed
who jerked awake, then stood to take a poop. Stooped
like that with paws gripping its knees, Mike looked like
a person in a poodle suit, but the poop was pure poodle.

"That's not how you spell 'fucking,'" I said, turning from his fox-
colored eyes, lit up bright enough to power the mower.
His was the uneven name of evening that would not
come back to bed 'til the work was done and done
right, about time too, so where were my garden gloves,
my shears? Make hey while the sun shines, etc.

THE CLIFFS ABOVE OSWALD

New fronds unfurl from the joints
of older ones, like fists slow to open
in forgiveness but will inevitably in
forgetfulness—that kind of newness green

as the green of new ferns snaking fast
up the old hosts' throats turning brown
beneath the ever-creep without a sound (to us—
all we hear's waves). The waist-high bramble

we're wading through, the thorn sea that has
swallowed us—with its endless view of day's
end/night's beginning—seems to seal up
behind us as we struggle by.

BAYWATCH

Like songs that say only
I like it like that or

I want my money back or
Back that thing up. "Dogs

peeing on people = funny.
People peeing on dogs = not

funny." That's a joke I stole
from a really dumb movie

I will remember—unlike my
mother's birthday—

for as long as I live.

Kiri Te Kanawa Singing "O Mio Babbino Caro"

When I was a younger thing, a voice unscarred
by scratches, growl or clashy wobble rung
cheesy in my ears—dippy—insincere. I'd go
off long and loud in dingy bars on Emmylou—
those 99.9% pure pipes moved my snide heart
less than Debby Boone. Angels were for Oprah—
give me wolves. Give me Callas, her final flailing
swipe at the rope—a yelp—before she tumbles
off the cliff. Give me Caballé, the wrecking ball—
her vengeance call, a roaring firehose of fat.

But this: only wide open *ah* and *oh*—bright as
knives but weightless as a prism-pitched rainbow—
clear Karo syrup, charmed (I'm sure), snaking
its way into cloudless blue sky—a cotton Cadillac
taking the curve magnet tight—no gap—cresting
the hill and not falling back to earth but flying off—
no roller coaster dip in the stomach—only more
air and *ooo*. Glitchless. *What's happening
to me?* I ask my parrot who has been lulled
to sleep by her sweatless, even song.

Love Poem: One Ton of Dirt

in sixty black garbage bags lined up on the walk
like dead seals. For seven hours, we shoveled bad
Brooklyn ground from the back bed where my flowers
wouldn't grow onto a tarp, turned, fertilized and re-
turned it all but one ton, which 311 says is Bulk
and must be disposed of one garbage bag at a time,
three times a week for twenty weeks. *Eesh.* Instead
we put an ad on Craigslist. There's nothing someone
isn't seeking. If a chump bites, this'll be the Mother
of all happy endings. Oh, hun, how we swung
wide from *Let's do it!* (me) à la Belushi, to *This sucks,*
to *This is where I get off,* to *We're gonna live* because
we are badass with shoulders sore, lower backs no
doubt rainbows of pain on the morrow. Careless heaves
with knees unbent and propensities to power through
don't bode well for our fifties. In the twilight your sweat-
soaked hair looks grayer than rain. I'm already up for
a tumble on Tuesday. Up on your toes for a goodbye kiss—
Freckles, AKA Blisters, you've never looked so tall
to me, sweat-brined, balk and all.

SLING AND MOLEY

Sling and Moley were at the beach
lying on a blanket under a tree. Nice.

They buried all their four feet deep
in the bluish sand. Cool. "Sling, I'm

hungry," said Moley. "I would be if I were
you," said Sling, "so why don't you wrangle

up grub like a real cowboy?" Moley
walked into the water, stuck his head

under, and inhaled it all into his lungs.
"Jesus Christ!" said Sling. Pearls,

plastic, and cans sat on the sand space
where ocean used to be. "I'm still hungry!"

cried Moley, so they gathered up some
pearls and sold them for big bucks

to a hoity-toity lady on the boardwalk:
"They match my diamonds divinely!"

They used some of the money to buy
french fries, and the rest a good house

under the same tree they'd started
under, then more fries. "You turned

out to be a lucky thing," said Sling.
"You never know what'll happen

with people," said Moley shaking
salt from his nose onto the plate.

NICE 'N EASY MEDIUM NATURAL ASH BRUNETTE

On their fifth date, Mike and Lou attended
a Grow Your Own Cocaine class at the Y.
All the young couples wanted to move some-
where with lots of mud, live in shacks where
rain swept in sideways, knit hybrid arugula
and grow their own cocaine. "We know how
to make wine in the toilet!" a scruffy couple
in matching T-shirts that said DIRT said
as the four hovered over the mirror. "I read that
after the apocalypse, potato chips will be extinct.
They're disappearing now," said Lou. "Good
riddance," said Scruffy gruffly which
saddened Lou for some reason. That night,
she asked Mike to strap on a Silver Spud before
they made love like animals, for hours, as some
wildly expensive thing in the oven burned.

ACKNOWLEDGMENTS

Thank you Charles Browning, Shanna Compton, Ada Limón, Sarah Manguso, Charlie Orr, Cam Roberts, Jason Schneiderman, and Deborah Stein.

Many thanks to the anthologies, journals and websites in which these poems have appeared or will appear, in one form or another:

Abraham Lincoln: Burt Reynolds FAQ, "M" Is for the Tears of Meat She Shed Me

The Agriculture Reader: Houston

American Poetry Review: Yellow Traces

The Awl: Baywatch, Saving Her Wasted Breath

Coconut: The Earth Is Flat and So's My Ass

Conduit: The Cliffs above Oswald, Dead Italians

Hotel Amerika: Cars

InDigest: Fat Cats, Skinny Rats

La Petite Zine: Beverly Hills Cop III, The Fattest Woman I Ever Loved, Seabirds

The Lifted Brow: All Her Dreams, Beloved Canadian Sandwiches, Don Ho's Funeral

LIT: Kiri Te Kanawa Singing "O Mio Babbino Caro," Old Friends

Loveless: Crawling Out of the Mouth of More

The Nepotist: The Mules of Death Valley, Marriage, A Coyote Walks into a Quizno's

No Tell Motel: Belle with a Showy Red Leak, Red/Green Colorblind Madness, Sling and Moley, You Are a Strategy

Octopus: The Atomic Weight of Grudges, "Coffee ice cream and Fruity Pebbles," Dirty Harry's Chrysalis, Nice 'N Easy Medium Natural Ash Brunette, One Man's Trash

Sixth Finch: Battle of the Network Stars: "Dream Team"

Tight: Modern Poetry, You're F*cking Crazy

Trnsfr: Anomalies of the Female Reproductive System

Vanitas: Lost Feet Swim in Backtracks Retraced

The West Wind Review: The Clean Underwear/Ambulance Thing

Photo credit: Jude Domski

Jennifer L. Knox was born in Lancaster, California—home to Frank Zappa, Captain Beefheart, and the Space Shuttle. Her other books of poems, *Drunk by Noon* and *A Gringo Like Me,* are also available through Bloof. A volume of her verse in German, *Wir Fürchten Uns,* is available through Lux Books. Her poems have appeared in three volumes of the *Best American Poetry* series, *Best American Erotic Poems, Great American Prose Poems: From Poet to Present,* and *Free Radicals: American Poets Before Their First Books.*

www.jenniferlknox.com

CPSIA information can be obtained at www.ICGtesting.com
Printed in the USA
BVOW05s1808200814

363535BV00003B/809/P